LOVE
LOVES
ME

LOVE
LOVES
ME

DEE WILLIAMS

XULON PRESS

Xulon Press
2301 Lucien Way #415
Maitland, FL 32751
407.339.4217
www.xulonpress.com

Unless otherwise indicated, Scripture
quotations taken from the King James Version
(KJV)–*public domain.*

Printed in the United States of America.

Paperback ISBN-13: 978-1-66280-580-6
eBook ISBN-13: 978-1-6628-0581-3

DEDICATION

This book is dedicated to my Lord and Savior, Jesus Christ. It is He who is the deepest love and joy of my life. I also dedicate this book to my mother, Marion Rosetta Johnson, who taught me to honor the Lord with my life. It was she who taught me to make Him first place. She is the one who instructed me to pray without ceasing and trust that He will answer. My mom coined the phrase "It doesn't hurt to say hello." as she, with a pleasant smile, spoke to everyone that she passed on the street. She invited traveling salesmen to dinner and much more. To my best friend and husband, Ben, of thirty-five years who has taught me in so many ways. There was a time that I used to embarrass you as I introduced you as my personal walking Bible Encyclopedia. You know me more than anyone else on earth—we have laughed and cried and everything in between together. I love you my buddy and partner in life. Thank you for allowing me to be simply crazy ole me. Also, to our three great children, who always encourage me to go for it. To John Michael, our self-proclaimed recipient of the double portion: You are so creative and special; your love for God warms my heart. Keep on being a chaser of God. To my shadow, Matthew Lawrence, never forget how wonderful you are. You have so much to offer this world. Keep on going beyond the standard and expect more for and from yourself. To Taylor Brooke Michelle—when I prayed for a baby girl, the Lord delivered in a most excellent way. It still amazes me that at your birth the doctors cried along in joy with us. I can honestly say that not even in the teen years, the three of you never caused us to lose so much as one night of sleep. Words cannot say how much I love you all. Each one of you is so vastly different from each other, but also in unison; you will always be the three amigos. To my heart-adopted daughter, Niima: From the moment that you laid your head on my chest, God supernaturally put you on the inside of my heart. To my dear sister Brenda—I miss you so much. Now in Heaven, you know just how incredibly beautiful you always were. To my baby sister, (Dr.) Poochie Dees, you are such a cheerleader in earnest;

you spur everyone on to be the best. You have such greatness on the inside of you. Also, to my big brother Louis: I missed so much of our life together so now I really love our Sunday dinners together. You are so funny and sweet natured at heart. Never quit striving to be all you can be, because you are so worth it to God and to us all.

For my mentor Pastor LaFrance Johnson—you taught me to never depart from the Word of God.

To some of the most lovely, loving, and humble people that I have ever met, Pastor James and Joyce Fennell

I cannot leave out the late Pastor George E. Hilton III and Stephanie, both will forever be in my heart.

TABLE OF CONTENTS

Chapters

FOREWORD

I met Dee at Church of the Firstborn in Delaware. After I was a member for about a year, she came over to me and said, "I have someone I want you to meet." I said, "I'm not interested." And if you know Dee, when she senses God telling her to do or say something she's not going to back down. Her reply, "Yes you are, I'll bring him to church next Sunday and we'll go out to dinner afterward." 28 years later she was right, I was interested. Dee has been friends with my husband Gregory for over ten years prior to me meeting him; they were like brother and sister. We became friends from that time forward, no sisters.

In my opinion, Dee's mission in life, which should be the mission of every born-again believer, is to make sure everyone she encounters knows that God loves them, and their need for Jesus. When we went out to eat, she would talk to the server about Jesus and pray for them—the manager too if he happened to come by. If we were in the store shopping, she would say to me I'm going to pray for the person and they would accept Jesus, tears and all. I remember a summer on Willow St. where we lived; it was considered the worse street in our area of town. Dee convinced me to join her in having our own Vacation Bible School in her backyard, Kings Kids. By the end of summer, we would baptize each kid—and some would praying in tongues. I thought, "Man, she ain't playin" Dee would say, "Come on, let's walk up and down our street and pray in the Spirit. We would get to the bar in the middle of the block and command it close in Jesus's name: It did. I remember one night we prayed for a neighbor out in front of our house with our husbands; he was very drunk. When Dee got done praying, he was quite sober. She told me the Lord wanted her to hold women conferences and said to me, "You're going to help me." She held her first one at the local library and then at a buffet restaurant a few times. She would help the waiters and waitresses be saved. They got so big we had to rent out conference rooms at hotels and God would show up every time. She started getting invites to churches to preach and other ministry engagements and I would be right there. When she taught the Word of God, I always learned something new. I love hearing her share the Gospel. She spends countless hours studying, praying, and fasting because she wants to be certain that you get all that the Lord wants to share through her. She actually fasted for forty days once. I didn't do that with her.

Little did I know the Lord had been preparing me for ministry through Pastor Dee Williams. When she teaches God's word, you sense how much God loves you.

That's what you are going to experience when you read this book. Dee loves God and she will do anything for Him. She is fearless, bold, funny, creative, smart, witty, talented, transparent, and anointed by God. This book will cause you to recognize how Love loves you.

Elder Rhonda L. Raines,
Principal, Urban Promise School
Wilmington, DE

PREFACE

I met the Lord when I was young, yet I knew by the age of twelve that I was called to preach the gospel. I remember feeling somewhat happy and loved at times. On the other hand, I also felt the sting of rejection at an early age. Being one of three girls, inside of myself I always felt compared. Compared to thin, compared to pretty, compared to smart. I was tall, they were all small; I was fat, they were thin; and the list goes on. I used to hate this women's clothing store named "5,7 and 9". I never fit any of those sizes. Talk about feeling isolated yet loved within the group of women in my family, especially so on our girl's day out for shopping trips. But boy how I did love those days out together, Mom, her sister Aunt Margaret, my sister-in-law to be Suzie, and my sisters Brenda, Poochie and I.

I used to read my Bible and sleep with it under my pillow. However, trying and failing to live out the do's and don'ts without recognizing the true love of the Father left me feeling disappointed with life and in myself. By not knowing my value, I accepted too many things and people in my world. I believed the word of others about me instead of truth. Finally, I grasped and understood the love of God—the love that He has clearly displayed in His Word to us.

I grew up not really realizing the effects of the absence of a non-absentee father. By this, I mean he was there, yet was not there, in the very same house. My father worked extremely hard, came home every night, and had his Schlitz every evening. He was there for every Christmas and every holiday, birthday, every cookout, and such. Yet, there was a void of real of relationship. So, I grew up wanting the attention of a daddy towards me. I cannot remember a time that he ever came to hear me sing at church, perform in a school play, or anything else where I personally shined. I grew up silently; then later, as a teen, outwardly angry at him. That anger translated to being "the mean one" within our household. I remembered being called upon to come fight for my older sister because I was supposed to be the one who didn't take no stuff. I now know that anger came from hurt and disappointment. It was more hurt than hate. I cannot remember a single time in my growing-up years that my father ever said the phrase, "I love you." As I look back, I am sure that he did love me but did not have the tools to verbalize such a thing. It was not until he was on his death bed, after accepting the Lord as his Savior, do I remember hearing him say the words, "I love you." As I remember, it that was a response to me saying it to him first. Present, yet absent.

I have found that parents were once children too, so they only live what they have learned. No judgment: he just was not that man. I had zero relationship with his mother, my grandmother, who lived only four doors down the street. Oddly, looking back he was not that close to her himself. I can joyfully say that I had a great mother who supported everything that I did; she was there for everything no matter what. My mom always told me how much she loved me and how pretty I was. She was self-sacrificing, gentle, but strict. She taught me to pray and love Jesus. She was my number one example of how to be kind yet stand up for something. My mom was the most gentle, sweet-hearted, tender person that I ever have known. I remember one time, my sister Brenda had a boyfriend who came to dinner. He asked to offer prayer over the food. He said a Muslim-directed prayer. When he finished, my mom very confidently said, "Now I will pray, because the Lord Jesus provided the food in this house." Then, she prayed. She went on to very graciously serve a delicious meal and that was that. She is so much of who I am, I wish I had more of her in me. Although my mother displayed her sacrificial love for me, just one encounter with

God the creator of the universe, LOVE HIMSELF changed everything. He allowed me to see that no matter to what extent others love or do not love me, LOVE loves me!

CHAPTER 1

WHAT'S LOVE GOT TO DO WITH IT? (EVERYTHING!)

Beloved, let us love one another, for love is from God, and whoever loves has been born of God and knows God. Anyone who does not love does not know God, because

GOD IS LOVE— (1 John 4:7–8 ESV)

According to this scripture, God does not merely operate in love or just have love; rather, **GOD is LOVE** and LOVE is GOD. We cannot have God and not have love, and neither can we have real love and not have God. The two are mutually inclusive. God's love language is Himself. When I awake in the morning, the first thing I do is acknowledge God the Father with a "Good morning, LOVE." I then remind myself that LOVE loves me just as I am. I breathe it in no matter what I am facing or how the tasks of the day ahead may appear. Then, I thank Him for just that. He loves me. He knows that I am not perfect, but He loves me anyway. I love Him in response to His great love, loving me first. I thank Him and praise Him before my feet hit the floor. I choose love and joy every day for my path and direction of my life.

> For God so loved the world, that he gave his only begotten Son, that whosoever believeth in him shall not perish,

but have everlasting life.
(John 3:16)

I would be remiss if I were to overlook the very beginning of this scripture: "For **God.**"

Most days, I will hear the phrase "Oh, God" or "OMG." In the ears of most, it is just white noise and means little. At times, His name is used in a reaction of shock, panic, or occasionally as a rant or rage in response to what is going on at that moment. The one that really affects me the most is when people very lightly say His name during a cursing fit. I can endure many

off-colored words, but that alone
is the one that grieves my heart. I
remember when I was a young, flip-
pant teen, I thought it was funny
to repeat what I had heard in the
streets, so I said, "God d***," while
talking to my mom about something. I was immediately met with a
smack across my mouth, and my lip
bled. Now, I have been about 5'8"
since about thirteen—when my
mother passed, she was all of 4'11",
which makes it even more of a statement now. She then apologized for
drawing blood but not for disci-
plining me about using God's name
in vain. She made it clear: we were

to never, ever speak in such a horrible light about our Awesome God. Do I need to say that was the very last time that I ever did? It was. It meant so much to me that growing up that I would warn my friends that cursing with God's name was over the line, and they curbed their speech too.

In Matthew 16 Jesus asked the disciples who do you call me? Though there are many gods according to the world, according to the Word—and my heart—there is only one God. It is He who is the Alpha and Omega, the beginning, and the end. There is only one that is the King of kings and Lord of lords.

He is known as Elohim,
my creator.
Jehovah, my Lord and God.
El Shaddai, the God of Plenty.
Adonai, my Master.
Jehovah Rapha, my Healer.
Jehovah Makeddesh, the Lord my
Sanctifier.
Jehovah Nissi, my Victory Banner.
Jehovah Jireh, my Provider.

Know that the LORD,
He is God; It is He who

made us, and not we our-
selves. (Psalm 100:3)

It is this very same all-powerful,
too-wonderful maker of Heaven
and earth God that loves us. **John
3:16 KJV "For God so loved
the world that he gave his only
begotten Son."**

One of the most noteworthy
attributes of love is giving. God
loved; God gave. If we are truly
walking in the God kind of love,
we cannot help but give, or at least
have a desire to give. Love gives.
True love that is from the heart
longs to give.

Real love-based giving is offering up something that might be precious or costly. Giving could be your time, attention, conversation, money, things, or sometimes, your own way. Love requires an action. Love is a verb. Love is something that you do not just say. True love gives. While love most eagerly gives, lust is looking to take. Love gives at your own expense and lust takes at another person's.

Many times, walking in love may not appear the way you would like. As I said, love gives at the expense of one's own self. I know that personally. I do not like to talk on the phone. First came the landline phone, which might as well have been called the landlocked phone. Do you remember the cordless telephone? Back in the day, I thought that would be my answer. It wasn't. Then there was the phone you could put on your hip with an earpiece. I hoped that was what I needed to be a successful phone communicator. That way, I could at least tend to the dishes, kids, and fixing dinner. *Yes, that must be my answer*, I thought. Nope. I finally realized I hate sitting still and talking on the phone. My eyes begin to wander to the dust on the shelf, the dinner that is not finished, the dishes in the sink, the conversations of my family in the background, and so on.

I got to the point I would never answer the telephone. When texting became a thing, I thought, *this is for me. I will text you, but I do not want to talk on the phone to you.* I would always rather have the company of my friends in person than speak to them on the phone. To be honest, I just don't focus well if we are not enjoying one another's company face to face. Texting allows me to read our conversations at my leisure and then respond. Although I will note that texting does not give the same inflection or excitement of a voice or a real person-to-person conversation. Then, one day while I was minding my own business, the Lord led me to **Hebrews 13:16: But to do good and to communicate forget not: for with such sacrifices God is well pleased**.

Oh, no, does that mean what I think it does? I gotta talk when I don't feel like it. I gotta answer the phone when I don't want to. I gotta make calls to let the people know that I love them too. Yes! Love is a giver. Love makes the sacrifice—even when we may not feel like giving by listening or talking.

So if I had to make calls from my driveway just to let the folks whom I love dearly know that they are important enough to call, I would willingly make and take the calls. That way, I would not get distracted by my family or the ever-calling tasks. God is still working on me in this area, but I have gotten better. A little better, Debbie?

Love does not necessarily tell us or give us what we want all the time. That is the wisdom that comes along with love. I thought about a local teen whose parent bought then a brand-new Mustang for a high school graduation gift. Very sadly that same week they were killed in a terrible crash. There are some things that we could destroy ourselves with if in our hands right when we want them. We do not have the right to throw a tantrum because we may not have gotten our way.

I remember once the Lord said to me, "Love sees the future and tells the truth." There are things that I know simply from age and experience that I warn our children about. They may huff and act like they choose not to hear. I remind them that Dad and I have been here a bit longer than they have.

Therefore, we just might know a little bit more than they do on this specific topic. I am not saying that we know it all, just some things. Many times, they tell us things that we did not know. I have found if you are humble enough you can receive instruction and knowledge even from a child.

According to **Proverbs 1:5, "A wise man will hear and increase in learning."** We can never get to the place where we think that we know it all because we do not. If we are all honest, there have been times when we did not want to deal with the truth about ourselves. As

in **James 1:19, "Be quick to hear,"**
or at least listen and weigh things
out and see if there is truth in what
you have heard about yourself. I
agree that the worst type of deception is self-deception, as according
to **James 1:22**. I invite you to take a
deep look into the mirror of God's
Word and get the reflection of how
you look in the light of the Word
of God. If you do not like what
you see, then receive His grace to
change into that image that He
knows that you can and should be.

God knew that I needed to hear
some things about myself because
He is omnipotent (all-powerful),

omnipresent (everywhere always), and omniscient (all-knowing). He can see down the road and knows what is best for me. He wants me prepared out of His love, not judgment. God is never wrong; the Bible says His word is truth. Love sees the future and tells the truth.

However, I do realize that if God pointed out all my errors at once, I would feel hopeless and worthless. Sometimes love is just sitting quietly. I have found over the years that I don't have to say everything that I think. **Proverbs 29:11 states, "A fool utters all of his mind, but a wise man keeps it**

in till afterwards." We do not have to prove that we are always right; sometimes, just be quiet. Love does not purposely cause injury. We must think before we say anything for **James 1:19** says to be **"slow to speak."**

CHAPTER 2

LOVE GIVES

Gift giving can be tricky. I love to give people gifts; I just do. Giving to others gives me joy. Have you ever bought something for someone because you really like whatever it is? I have. It was not because I wanted it for myself. It was more because I had hopes that they would like it as much as I did. At times, that can be selfish giving.

I think that giving out of love is searching for something that the person would really appreciate— something that is their taste, style, desire, or need. Sometimes, we must listen for clues when people are talking about what they would like. Also, take mental notes when at the mall or having conversations. What excites the person that I am getting a gift for? If it is for Rhonda, think green; if it is Regina, think purple; and so on. In the early years, my husband and I bought some misguided, even laughable gifts for each other. From those experiences, I learned to tuck away in my memory what makes others excited. I have found that gadgets light my husband up. It can be many months until a holiday, but frequently I already know what I want to surprise him with. That is how God loves us. What is important to you is important to Him.

I have an amazing sister, Poochie. She and I love each other and were both born on October 26—the same day but six years apart. Yes, I am the elder. We both have a strong appreciation for Trader Joe's coffee ice cream with fresh pecans on top. However, when it comes to personal style, I like baroque-inspired big diamonds, big bracelets, earrings, and the like. I like orange, hot pink, and bright colors everywhere. I have never needed to rock a name brand because brands don't impress me. Now, if it is a piece that I really admire and it just happens to have some designer's name attached, that is a different story.

Poochie is more drawn to turquoise and blues. She is much more petite and delicate than I am, so she likes petite rings, bracelets, and jewelry and prefers pastel tones. She is very classic and classy—almost Jackie O themed. I sometimes might see something that I think is amazing, only to find she is like, "Okay." We admire some similar things, but some things just would not be for the other. Sometimes I think, *what could you possibly see in that small, unnoticeable pair of earrings?* I carry a big head along with my large personality, so little earrings do nothing for me; that goes for lovely diamond rings too! (Honey, feel free to upgrade often. Sorry, I diverted a bit.) Anyway, she has great taste, but I think I do too. I am the artist of the family, and things catch my eye that would never catch Poochie's and vice versa. With each passing year, Poochie and I learn more and more what the other likes. This is because what is important to her is important to me and what is important to me is important to her. We race every year to see who can get a birthday gift or card in the mail and have it delivered first. Sometimes I cheat and mail it on October 1. She won the birthday race this year.

Now I work to find things that speak to her, no matter whether I am personally draw to them. A fitting example was this past year at Christmas: she bought and mailed me the most amazing necklace. I am really over the moon about it.

It is so pretty and big and a real statement piece. The funny thing is the more she looked at it as she wrapped it up to send to me, the more she liked it for herself too. She went back to where she bought mine, but they were sold out. She then traveled a bit and found one for herself. Now we both have one. So now we were birthday twins and necklace twins.

Love is giving the gift that the other person would appreciate or need. Look back and think about yourself. How do you love? How does the love that you have received appear to you? Can you honestly say that you have put your best foot of love forward? We will not always get it right but we can try. There are times where we have just settled for what we thought love to be. To be honest, we have all given or received self-centered love.

We have all endured a poor love show at some point. Aim to not to be a people pleaser, taking whatever comes along. For example, I have a good friend who is looking for a wife. He refuses to marry someone just because they are also a single Christian with no kids. Know and walk in your truth that lines up with the Word of God for you.

Some people do not want to know the truth; they are satisfied just settling. Of course, the next sentence is improper use of the English language, but you can grasp what I am saying. Are you a ... "just don't wanna know" type of person?

Rock the love boat and look a bit deeper than the surface. Don't be afraid to have those conversations with yourself and the originator of love, God. You deserve to love and be loved. The fear of what others think will keep you trapped right where you are. I have written on my vision board, "Expect more for yourself, and expect more from yourself."

I was once recording a teaching, and right smack dab in the middle of speaking about loving something, the Lord spoke clearly inside of me and said, "Love is for people, not things."

Too often we make statements like,

"I love those shoes!"

"Girl, that dress is all that; I love it!"

"Honey, look at that car! I love it!"

"I love her lasagna; it is the best!"

And so on, and so on, and so on, saying what we love, spewing out the things that we love. Quit using the *love* word for everything because it loses its value when we use that word in earnest. I also have learned to quit referring to anything as awesome. There is truly only One that is Awesome! So, I reserve that phrase for Him alone.

God said to me, "Love is for people." Love is for people because God loves people, not things. We are to direct our love toward people and God. Do not love and worship the self-set idols of things.

Love not the world, neither the things that are in

the world. If any man love the world, the love of the Father is not in him. For all that is in the world, the lust of the flesh (it feels good), **and the lust of the eyes** (it looks good), **and the pride of life** (inordinate self-worth), (this) **is not of the Father** (LOVE), **but is of the world. And the world passeth away, and the lust thereof: but he that doeth the will of God abideth for ever.** (1 John 2:15–17) (parentheticals added)

Things are temporary, but people and God are eternal. Things do not have power to heal you, save you, or love you in return. No matter what the thing is, do not allow it to become an idol. Too many people get their self-worth in what they drive, where they live, or what designer they have on their back, bags, or shoes. If your house burned to the ground along with your brand-new luxury car and worldly possessions, how would you feel about you afterward? During financial crises, people have committed suicide because they lost, in a sense, themselves. It was reported in a study in the USA Today that at least 10,000 or more Americans and Europeans committed suicide between 2007-2010. It is believed to be connected to the financial crisis around that same time. They equated their monetary worth with their personal self-worth and lost it all. I see this in ministry too. We get so caught up in the ministry and preaching, teaching, and singing that sometimes we forget why and for whom. The Lord told me, "Before there was a call, there was an us." He is now the sole reason that I do what I do, but even if I do not do it, LOVE still loves me.

If we are disloyal, he
stays faithful, because
he can't be anything
else than what he is.
(2 Timothy 2:13 CEB)

I thought to myself, proving out
what I heard. Would I give my life
for someone's lasagna? Would I
really kill for those shoes? Would I
give my life for that car or that dress?
Of course not! Let your words have
power in saying what you mean and
meaning what you say. Sometimes I
slip up and catch myself. I must stay
on myself too. There are times that I
have to remind myself and say, "No,

no, no, I like that or admire that thing, but I do not love it. Love is for people. Love is for God."

Picture someone coming up to you with a gun and saying, "Give me your purse or wallet with the cash and credit cards." You most likely would say, "Here, take it, take it all, and here are my pass codes and pin numbers too." I am employed at a car dealership, and I sometimes have customers tell me how they had an accident, and their vehicle was totaled. I often tell them, "I am glad you are okay." I go on to tell them, "Thank God you are here to tell the tale." Live to tell the tale. Give up your money, not your life.

Now let us look at the same scenario, but this time it is your spouse, kids, or other loved ones. If you are anything like me and most people, you would fight with all that you have to protect and save them. So when the rubber meets the road, did you love those things? No! Why else would you not fight so hard for stuff? You can always regain and replace things. Do you love those people? Absolutely yes! People cannot be replaced. Again, love is for people, not things.

CHAPTER 3

IT'S OKAY TO HAVE A LITTLE SOMETHIN' -SOMETHIN'

I have shewed you all things, how that so laboring ye ought to support the weak, and to remember the words of

the Lord Jesus, how he said, It is more blessed to give than to receive. (Acts 20:35 KJV)

Although it is wonderful to be a giver, do not for one moment think that you are not to be a receiver too. It is okay to have things. Another part of my daily confessions of faith is "I love to give, and I am quick to receive. Jesus is my overrunning supply." I don't understand the teaching from our Catholic brothers along with the nuns, how they make a vow of poverty. I totally understand how they take the vow of chastity and the vow of obedience. I am all for obeying the Lord. But that vow of poverty thing is not in accordance to the scripture that I can see. If the earth is the Lord and we are his children, in serving and obeying him and with all that we know, living for him, we are to have things. I am not speaking of this new age of the entitlement belief. There are certain portions of the body of Christ that believe that we should be poor and destitute and give away everything that we own. Mull this over with me. Not for one moment should we get things twisted as some people in the body of Christ often do. Although love is for people, not things, our loving Father wants us to have and enjoy things. God wants you to have things. Multiply the joy that you get giving to your kids by ten thousand or more and know that your Father God gets even more joy in giving to you.

Let the LORD be magnified, who delights and takes pleasure in the prosperity of His servants. (Psalm 35:27 **AMP**)

Charge those who are rich in this world that they be not haughty, nor trust in uncertain riches, but in the living God, who gave us richly all things to enjoy. (1 Timothy 6:17)

It makes God happy to see us enjoy good things; just don't love them. Don't make them your god. My son John shared a word from the Lord that he received, and my spirit agreed immediately. He said that the Lord said to him, that because he does the right thing with money (ie. sowing, tithing, obeying when prompted to give) that now he can do what he likes with money.

Until you are in the position to give, you will never really know the joy that comes with giving. I personally can get jump-up-and-down joy from giving a great gift. I know firsthand giddy joy. My husband works and has worked ridiculously hard for our family for years. So, this year I wanted to surprise him, so I bought him a brand-new favorite blue car. I had a bow on it and had it parked in the driveway when he arrived home. I was so excited to give it to him that I almost went to meet him at work with it. I just remembered thinking how much I wanted him to feel the love of me and the love of God. In his easy manner he was just calmly strolling to the car in a slow-moving shock. God is even more giddy with joy from giving to us. The Bible says it pleased the father to bruise Jesus. That was because it would birth the church. The Word goes on to say that Jesus himself peered into the future, past the suffering of the cross for the joy set before Him. The church, His joy!

Again, God Almighty wants us to have things. He does not,

however, want things to have us. God does not expect us to be snobbish or stuck up because of the things that he has allowed us to have. I repeat, do not make things your gods.

We have been given the Old and New Testament. Together they are the written will of God. A will and testament are a legal document written and signed telling of what is to be passed on after the death of the testator. Jesus died and left His written will for us. Jesus signed this will in His own precious blood. If we believe the will, all that is within

it is ours. We were left some awesome promises in that will.

I was taught the Lord's Prayer in
my childhood. We repeat it a most
funerals, including all denomination affiliations. We say it by rote.

**After this manner there-
fore pray ye: Our Father
which art in heaven,
Hallowed be thy name.
10 Thy kingdom come,
Thy will be done in
earth, as it is in heaven.
(John 6:9)**

We are all praying in unison with Jesus, many times without realizing it. We are praying, "Father God, let Your will be done on earth in the exact manner as it is in heaven." What is the exact manner of heaven you may ask? Jesus Himself taught this prayer. Jesus is telling us to pray and receive all the access of heaven to be ours here on earth—not in the sweet by and by, but in the blessed here and now.

A few years ago on the very same day that my mother Marion R. Johnson moved to heaven, my son had what is known as an opened vision, An opened vision is when

God will pull back the natural view of this world to show us something else that he wants us to see. It can appear like you are looking at a movie screen. In this opened vision he told us how he saw the ceiling in the living room disappear and the sky open to see into heaven. He saw my mother who was blind and in her 80's, dancing, twirling and praising God with her full eyesight. God is real and heaven is an actual place.

What does heaven have? Heaven has total healing and health. There is not one sick person in heaven—no, not one. That makes my heart rejoice. When I think of my loved ones there, they are brand new and whole, no pain, no suffering, not worried about anything at all. What does Heaven look like? The streets are paved with gold (so I don't think having bling on your finger and neck are outside of God's will). The gates are made of pearls. Go read in **Revelation 21:18–19** about just what Heaven looks like.

Once again, I say that God Almighty wants us to have and enjoy things. Perhaps you, like I, may have read about, sang about, or heard something for years, but when the Lord says it to you, it is like lightning shooting through you, an aha! moment. It was this way for me when the Lord let me know that He wants me to have. Not just have, but to abundantly have.

I always understood the concept that He wanted me to have enough to get along—enough to pay my bills, have a car, buy some food, and dress. Ponder this: God wants his children to give out of the overflow, the more than enough, the too much for just me. God is the El Shaddai, the God of too much. How selfish it is to think of *I want just enough*. I have heard people say, "I don't want to be rich, but just enough to get along enough for me." Lies! Of course, we should be grateful to have enough. However, if I have just enough, I cannot help anyone else except for me and mine, and sometimes not even mine. I cannot cover your car payment if I can barely pay my own. What a sad existence that is. Allow things and money to become tools to show love, not the love of money or things. Love is for people.

The Lord spoke to my heart and said, "I have already given you my very best in that I gave you Jesus, my Son. So, daughter, why wouldn't I want you to have?" "Daughter, it ain't no thing to give you things." When will we grasp that the King of kings is our father? Say this with me now. "I am the King's son/daughter, I am a royal I will show forth His praise in every area and arena in my life. Then my mind was quickened back to the scripture:

He that spared not his own Son but delivered him up for us all, how shall he not with him also freely give us all things. (Romans 8:32)

The Son is so much more valuable than the "all things." So, if God gave us His Son Jesus, the things are easy to get into your hands. Plus, when you study this out, the etymology of "all things" means ALL THINGS! Duh!

I love my husband!

I love my family!

I love my friends!

But a thing is just a thing!

It is time for us to freely receive all things from our Father.

If threatened, even my favorite necklace from Poochie can be found somewhere again. I appreciate it, I admire it, I like it, but I don't love it. I love her.

I feel a song coming on. "It don't mean a thing just because it has bling, doo wah, doo wah, doo wah, doo wah, doo wah, doo wah, doo wah, doo wah!"

Look at the birds of the air; they neither sow (a seed) **or reap** (the harvest) **nor gather** (the crops) **into barns, and yet your heavenly Father keeps feeding them. Are you not worth much more**

than they? (Matthew 6:26 AMPC)

You are worth *much more* than any old bird. I researched the most expensive birds in the world. On the aviary conservation list, I found that the racing pigeon comes in at number one. Yes, it tripped me out too. The world's most expensive bird is the racing pigeon? Can you believe that?. It is valued from $90 thousand up to one that sold in 2013 for $6 million. You are worth more, much more, and you are better looking too.

Having fresh flowers on my nightstand, kitchen, or living room adds to my joy. Flowers are so pretty, and some smell so good. My favorites are lilacs. The aroma of a lilac bush is what I imagine heaven will smell like—that or Amazing Grace by Philosophy, a perfume that was my mom's signature scent. Matthew 6:27-29 goes on to say how flowers do not work hard or spin wool to sew ornate fabrics in order to be dressed in their beauty. Their wardrobe is God given. They are dressed better than one of the wealthiest men on earth, that being King Solomon. Yet again your heavenly Father decks them out, and they smell great. (Side note, your worship has a fragrance before the throne.)

In verse 26, the phrase "yet your heavenly Father" stands out to me. That says I am his child; birds and flowers are just his creation. Why would my Daddy take care of a bird and not me? What kind of a father would feed the bird in the park down the street and let his very own child go without? That would be a bad father. Please know that God is a good father. Have you seen a skinny, undernourished bird barely flapping around for want of food?

Every time we see a bird, we need to lift a "thank you Jesus." When you see a beautiful flower, remember to say, "God, you are good," and "LOVE loves me!"

Yes, it is God's pleasure for us to prosper with things, but we are not to seek after things but seek the Lord, who gives all good things. We do not just want the arm of the Lord, but we want to seek the face of the Lord. His arm speaks of His strength and what he can do for us. The Hebrew word for face in the Old Testament is paniym which refers to His presence and His countenance. If we look for His presence, all His goodness comes along with it by faith.

CHAPTER 4

HE THAT GIVES ALSO FORGIVES

The same God that gives is the same Love that forgives. Grasp this truth on the inside of your heart and mind now and never, ever forget it. The God that gives freely, forgives just as freely. Forgiveness was not free, but it was already paid for by the precious blood of

Jesus. God so loved the world that he gave us Jesus, He also forgave us. Forgiveness for all that you have ever done wrong. Every sin that you have ever committed, forgiven. Not only past sins but he has already forgiven your future sins. The blood of Jesus does not wax old. The blood of Jesus is always as fresh as the sinner needs it to be. The blood of Jesus is still on the mercy seat in heaven defending making a defense for us. His blood cries innocent on our behalf in the court of heaven and on the behalf of anyone who receives it. All we ever need do is ask Him. He hears and He forgives.

Pray this aloud with me now. "**Most gracious heavenly Father. You are the Most High and I ask you to forgive me of all my sins. I ask you to cleanse me. My hearts cry is for Jesus to be my Lord and Savior. I now receive the gift and sacrifice that God gifted through Jesus. Make me new and heaven ready. I believe that Jesus is the Son of God, who gave His life for me. Jesus, come into my heart and save me from sin and unrighteousness. Thank you, Lord, that I am forgiven. I receive all that you have for me in this life and the life to come. In Jesus's name. Amen.**"

You have now moved from a mere creation of God into a child of God. You are now part of the family of God through Christ Jesus.

Although God loves the world and all the people in the world, everyone is not His child automatically. There are two groups of people in the world: The children of God and the children of the devil. There are some who have self-elected to be the child of the devil some knowingly and some unknowingly. It does not take doing something so horrible that you become the child of the devil. You do not have to join up with a cult, nor worship the devil to belong to him. It can simply be that a person has not believed and accepted Jesus' complete and finished work on the cross. He did it to take our place, He paid for our sins. Think of it this way, someone buys you a brand-new car, shiny, sporty, just what you like and need and you refuse to take the keys. It will sit there until it rusts. It is paid for, it is yours however it is your choice to receive it. If you don't choose Jesus the Bible **says "You are of your father, the devil...his works will you do. (John 8:44).** If you choose not to take the keys, keep on walking. When you do not accept Jesus as your Savior you are on the same level spiritually as a devil worshipper. It is not what you do, it is who you choose. It is more about who you choose or reject. The choice is yours. Everyone must opt-in to belong to the family of God. When we opt-in to be in God's family, we have opted out of belonging to the devil's family. Anyone can be part of the family of God if they choose to be. So, when I hear people say, "But I just can't believe." No, it is more like they just choose not to believe. The Bible says in **(Romans 12:3) "God hath dealt to every man the measure of**

faith." What you do with the measure that you have been given is your choice. You just choose Jesus, to be in the family of God. You can choose to utilize the faith given toward a false god or religion. I try not to knock someone for believing in some other god. I think that their faith is just misdirected. My job is to get it pointed in the right directions, not kick them for believing something. Faith is from God. If you prayed that prayer to receive Jesus from your heart of hearts, you are now His child through faith. Welcome to the family!

Have you ever heard this phrase? I can forgive you, but I will never forget what you did. I still remember how you made me feel when you did what you did. Forgiveness is a command from God, but it is up to us to obey it. We are commanded to forgive, so that we can be forgiven. Forgive, so that your prayers can be received. The Word of God says this is how God forgives. **"...as far as the east is from the west, so far hath He removed our transgressions from us" (Psalms 103:12).** I understand that east and west like the orb of a desk top globe, do meet. However, in real time the east and the west never meet again. East and west are to infinity and beyond. In **Micah 7:18-19** also goes on to say that He places our sins into the sea of forgetfulness. Now, find that sea on the map. If you can find that sea you can find your sins. Guess what? God said He will forget your sins forever and never bring them up to you again. Forever is a long time. He will not bring your former sins nor throw them in your face.

**"Love keeps no record
of wrongs."
(I Corinthians 13:5
NIV)**

Erase these questions from your mind, "will God bless me; will God hear me, because I sinned so many times how could he"? In the eyes of God, your confessed sins and forsaken sins do not exist and never did exist. DO NOT and NEVER DID exist!

God does not bless us based on us but, on Himself. God blesses us based on the blood that Jesus shed for us. It is his heart to give and forgive. Your sins never remembered by God again. Now hear this, the enemy called the devil will remember. He loves to throw what you did wrong up into your own face. He is also called the accuser of the brethren. He will make accusations about you to you, and about you to others, and to you about others. **John 10:10-11 The thief** (Hater and devil) **only comes to steal and kill and destroy. I** (Jesus) **came that you may have life and have it more abundantly. I** (Jesus) **am the good shepherd. The good shepherd lays down his life for the sheep."** The devil is a liar; the Bible calls him the father of lies. He will also use others to remind you of that time that you did that dirty deed, in that dirty way, way back in 19...whatever. Just like our **Father**

God is Love. The devil is Hate (he does not even deserve a capital "d"). He hates you, he hates me, and he hates whole world. Nowhere near as much as I hate him. Hark, I feel another song rising *"the devil and I, we both agree, I hate him, and he hates me, all of my sins are washed away, I've been redeemed"*. The Hater hates us because we are in the image of God. However, he is defeated foe. Shut him up and let him know that in Jesus's name that you have been forgiven, and it is more than merely forgiven all your sins forgotten. Now that God Almighty has forgiven you, forgive yourself and move on. Say it loud and say it proud, "I am forgiven by God, so I forgive myself!"

I know for my own household there was a time that everything turned into an argument, I mean everything. I spent time praying about it and the Lord gave me a revelation that stays with me until this day. The Lord said that strife is a spirit. That spirit (from the Hater) sits around waiting for someone to engage it. Someone must take up with it for it to operate. **Proverbs 26:20 NKJV "Where there is no wood, the fire goes out."** Don't allow yourself to become the wood to get the fire roaring. All strife needs to incite a riotous atmosphere is a response from another. **Proverbs 15:1 NKJV "A soft answer turns away wrath, but a harsh word stirs up anger."** Strife brings along with it his lying friends of provocation (action or speech that provokes or goad to anger especially deliberately), contention (heated disagreement), sedition (inciting rebellion), and disunion (the breaking up of relationships). If we permit it to, it turns into a strife of tongues, warring with words against the very ones that we love more than anyone in the world.

Fighting to be right just ain't right! In my very own family, we all could go at it and never use one foul word. My husband and my daughter are alike. They have a hidden lawyer in them that want to fight just for a good debate. They will work to prove you wrong even if they know that you a completely right. They will take it to the letter of the law just to win the war. They will work to sway you to their side, right or wrong. They sometimes will laugh at the end and say, "I just wanted to watch you go." Our oldest son and I are alike—we fight for what we really think is right. We will have facts and figures that we believe to be true. We see very black or white, with very few gray areas. Either way strife is strife, and it leads to hurt feelings on the part of someone. I can tell you that the Hater aka the devil loves it. He loves it because as my mentor Pastor LaFrance always says, "words are like bullets, and you can shoot them out, but you cannot take them back." I now recognize his tactics and have learned to bind the Hater in Jesus, name. We are not perfect but praise God, we have improved greatly. I can say this of each of us, we are quick to forgive.

Just like God did for you do for others, forgive. Act like God, and do like Nike, "Just Do It!" Know that the offender can never pay you back for what they have done to you, just like we could never pay God back for what we have done. Neither they nor we could ever be sorry enough to travel back in time to take it back the offense that was committed. Unforgiveness holds you back from being all you can be. I like a statement Oprah Winfrey had to say about forgiveness. "Forgiveness is giving up the hope that the past could have been any different." So, with or without another's apologies, forgive knowing that your Heavenly Father has forgiven you. Forgiveness! Pass it on.

Join me in one of my daily confessions "I am quick to forgive"

The voice of the Lord once said this to me. "The story that you continue to tell becomes, **your** stronghold." A stronghold is a fortress, or a fortified place that cages **you** in. A stronghold can be a good thing in a sense, or it can be detrimental. If we keep telling ourselves that same old story how they did us wrong, how they lied on us, how they cheated us, whispered about us, then we are the ones that will remain caged in. The longer that you nurse it and rehearse it, it will keep you right there caged in with that same pain and torment as you relive it. How many more time do you need to tell that story to feel better? How many more people do you have to share your misery and pain with before you feel better about it? Allow me to help you, you cannot tell it enough and it get better. You cannot regurgitate it enough to get healing from it. Jesus is the healer; therefore, don't expect another's apologies no matter how sincere they might be, to heal you. Even if they want their apologies to heal you, they never will. Their words can't heal you. Eventually, what will happen is that others, who must repeatedly hear your stories of woe, will begin to shy away from you. Why would they want to be locked inside your fortress with you? People will begin avoiding you like the plague. Don't let the story become who you are. You have so much more to offer than that same old story. You cannot even attain your future if you are stuck in the hurt filled prison of your past. It is impossible to move forward successfully if you keep looking backward. Try walking a city block facing backwards. Number one, you will look really strange. It will take you much more time to get to your destination. Then you will most likely stumble along your way, you might possibly fall. When God instructed Lot in **Genesis 19** to flee Sodom and the 4 surrounding cities, he told him and his family through the angels do not even look back. **Remember Lot's wife?** She looked back and turned into a pillar of salt because of her disobedience. When you keep looking back and reliving your past, you become as a salt pillar so to speak. You become stuck in that time; you will begin to crumble under that stronghold of pain. When we use our words telling and retelling the same old story, it deepens the grooves and scars in our mind, memory. I also thought about the apostle Paul when he said, ***"...but this one thing I do, forgetting those things that are behind, and reach forth unto those things which are before. I press toward the goal..."*** (*Philippians 3:13-14*). You cannot successfully press toward the goal if you don't leave the past in the past. You may need to tell your story and get the proper counseling from a trusted friend or even a professional. If they are good at what they do they will help you to move to the next place. Together set a day and time to tell that story for the last time in defeat. Cry it out if you need to. If ever you need to tell it again let it only be a testimony of the victory that you have achieved, in order to help someone else reach the freedom that you have obtained.

Chapter 5

Sing a Brand-New Song

I appreciate many types of music and songs that have been written over the years. However, there is only one way that I like worship music served up. Well done. I know that the word worship comes from the Greek word (proskuneo)

that means to bow and to kiss.
Worship should be about bowing
to our King and kissing toward the
Son Jesus. So many Christian music
songs that are called worship are
everything but worship. Too many
songs could be sold under Damon
Johns designed label, **FUBU**. It
seems that Increasingly that I
hear songs that seem to be "**For
Us, Bout Us**". By this I mean that
songs are about the works the devil
has been up to, but not about what
God has done. Have you ever heard
a well-meaning testimony, where
a person stands up, with all good
intentions, to tell the goodness of

our God? I have heard people go on and on about all the devil did to them. Nobody knows the trouble I've seen. Then somewhere at the end they may throw in, but God delivered us, amen. They gave 5 minutes to the Hater and 5 seconds to Love. True worship should be about Him and for Him. Christian songs without Jesus as the focus are just emotional entertainment. Our words in song should be extolling and exalting Him. Worship songs need to be full of the Word of God. Songs that give Him alone glory honor and praise not the enemy.

Begin to repeat and speak over yourself a brand-new song. Sing and speak according to what the Word of God says about you. We cannot keep singing the same ole somebody done somebody wrong song and expect change on the inside. I do not want to sound or appear unsympathetic, but it is time for a new story with new glories. You may think "well just how do I move on"? Stop with the old and start fresh and new. You cannot battle a thought with a thought. But you can win the war of thoughts with your words. Begin with your words. Say something different. No longer allow yourself to sing the same sad song. When I wake up and I feel the least bit of sadness try to come on me, I know it's time to start talking. I begin to say who I am, whose I am, what I can have, what I can do through Christ who strengthens me. I cast out the spirit so sorrow, sighing and sadness to flee away in Jesus's name. I stand against oppression, depression anger or fear. It takes a few minutes sometimes, but it always goes. Less and less do I ever need to deal with it. There is no use stopping bad old habits if you do not replace them with great new ones. When you stop with the sad story, begin telling a new story. Let your mind be transformed and reformed, tell good new stories and victories. Tell stories of how you are blessed. Tell of the favor that you had shown to you. Tell how you have made it to where you have made it to today. Share the visions for your future victories. ***Romans 12:2 "...be ye transformed by the renewing of your mind."*** Tell tales of what you are expecting and thankful for. Make for yourself a positive stronghold with the gratefulness, praise, words and promises of God. Think on what has been great and what will be better.

It may take some doing to remind and stop yourself mid sad story. Dig new grooves in your mind. Imagine all the goodness that is stored up for you. God gave you an imagination. Picture yourself where you want to be. I used to tell my one co-worker, smile on purpose. That trick alone sends signals to your body and raises your emotions to a better place. It has been proven that smiling even if it is fake releases hormones in your body of happiness. Think of your future life from today forward. Think about what kind of a person that you are meant to be? Envision how you'd like to dress, what you will drive, where do you want to live? Don't just think it, ink it. **Habakkuk 2:2 "Write the vision and make it plain..."**

Let us take a short journey back in this whole thing for a moment.

John 3:16 "For God so loved the <u>world</u>..."

In this time and temperature of the nations, we need to know that LOVE loves the world. God did not just love white people; God did not just love black people, nor Asian people, Mexican or Indian people, but the entire world. God loves, gay people, straight people, fornicators, adulterers, single, married, children, adults—the whole gamut. God so loved the world! God did not send His Son just to save America. God sent Jesus to be the savior of the world.

I never could get racism. It is an evil hurtful spirit. It is also a very stupid spirit and those that ascribe to it. It is hard to o think that someone would think that because of a basal layer of the skin, the slant of an eye, or the curl of hair makes one better than the other. How dumb a devil is that and they that follow such nonsense are just as dull witted as he is. It is the truth that at on the cross Jesus crushed his skull. There is really no excuse for them.

When I see fools, (that is a deep Bible term) do things such as burn crosses in the name of the Lord, it deeply bothers me. The Bible says that a fool says in his heart that there is no God. They are right, for them they have made the Hater their god. So, in essence there is no real God for them. Foolishly, they are thinking that they are representing the God who loves the world. No, rather they are representing what the Bible calls the god of this world,

Satan. **You belong to your father, the devil, and you want to carry out your father's desires. He was a murderer from the beginning, not holding to the truth, for there is no truth in him.** (**John 8:44**) **NIV** You cannot have eternal life with the Father of Love and be so filled with hatred. Love loves the world and all the people of it. Love loves them too; they just have not received it yet. Just like God is equal to love. The devil is equal to hate. Remember this, for Hate so hates the world. The Hater loves bigotry, prejudice division and pride. The Hater even hates the people that call themselves devil worshippers. He does not care about them at all they are still made in the image of God. He just wants to keep them deceived long enough to lose their shot at eternal life.

There are denominations that work like that too. Believing if you are not part of us you are not part of the body of Christ. There are those hating their brothers and sisters because they may or may not speak in other tongues, or worship like we worship, or dress like we dress. I do not believe in what every old body calls a "church" is of Jesus. As it has been said before just because it has a huge arched "M" hanging outside does not make it sell hamburgers inside. I do not agree with so-called churches that have changed the Word of God to fit their conscience—attempting to conform God's word to the world standards instead of vice versa. I reject that spirit of the antichrist. Yup! I love you and love tells the truth. The worst deception in life is to be self-deceived. These are all types of schisms. A schism is division between people, a split a rupture or a break. This is how all the various denominations of Christian churches have come about. I got into my heart a long time ago that I can visit and worship at any church denomination if they name the name of Jesus Christ as Savior and Lord. They may sing different songs, clap on a different beat, run around or just sit down. If they are reading God's Word, I can get something out of it. Love can fellowship with the family no matter what building the family worships in. If you should fall into any of these categories where you just can't find something to agree on, ask the Lord to cleanse your heart and to remove all the blinders from your mind of the isms, (racism, classism, denominationalism, sexism and all other schisms) and ask God to help you to love like He loves.

The Lord God will receive everyone and anyone who comes to Him with a pure and humble heart. Understand that the darker the sin, the brighter His love that is shining toward a person. It is never too late to begin a new life with Him.

Believe the love. Love loves you.

I think of the beautiful hymn Just As I Am by Charlotte Elliot. "Just as I am without one plea in that Thy blood was shed for me and that thou bid'st me to come to Thee O Lamb of God I come! I come!"

As Love invites us into changing, change by His grace and ability. We must make disciplined habits to grow. Overall, it will be by His power through attending to the Word of God. The blood of Jesus will do any fixing if we yield to receive. Never think that you can fix yourself or you would have done it long ago.

Your personal goodness does not make God love you. He already did and does love you. **Romans 5:8 But God demonstrates His own love toward us, in that while we were yet sinners, Christ died for us.** Before we could think to be good or bad, before we could lift one finger to be anything, God loved us. Understand this, God out of His very own goodness decided to be good to us and love us. The God kind of love is a word in the Greek, agape, the highest form of love. Love for no reason, the perfect love of God was shown to us. There is no reason not to accept it. Love is a gift. God's love is free to us. Now while love is a gift, trust is earned. Make yourself trustworthy of the love given freely to you. God's love for us is so great that he would never force us to love him back. Do you know that God Almighty respects you? He allows us to have the power of choice. God respects your decision.

> **Come unto me all you who labor and are heavy laden and I will give you rest. Take my yoke upon you and learn of Me;"** *Matthew 11:28-30.*

The issues of life are too heavy for you to carry. Life is full of self-conviction, hatred, depression, oppression, fear, failure, loss, lack, sickness, grief, and self-hatred. (God's love yoke is bearable and full of love. The Lord is saying let us have a great exchange. I will take your burdens and give you the anointing yoke that I carry. Love is saying let me do in you and for you what you cannot do for yourself. Love is saying "here take the sweet rest that I have already completed for you on Calvary." Now Jesus's victory becomes our victory. Take it! Hallelujah for the great exchange!

Not until we realize just how much the God of the universe loves us, can we comprehend that we are worthy of being loved by others or loving ourselves. I personally had a low self-worth, not knowing exactly who I was or what I deserved in life. I didn't know which way to go or what to do. I did not know what I should expect for myself, I just let life happen. Days just turned into years as I thought they just should. No goals, no plans, just living day to day. There were things that I thought I'd like to achieve but somehow, I thought that I couldn't. What a lie, I now know that I could have been anything that I wanted to be.

No matter how seemingly brave or bold some may want to appear to others, each one of us at some time have faced some form of insecurity. It could be a lack of ability, or our appearance, our low economic status or something as simple as the fear of standing before a room to speak. The key thing is not to allow the fear, and insecurities to intimidate then paralyze us. One of the most enlightening things that I heard from Joyce Meyers once was "do it afraid"! So, with knees knocking, heart pounding, sweat forming, stomach churning and lips quivering, dare yourself to move forward. One step at a time, always inching forward, knowing that Love's got your back. **I John 4:18 NAS "...perfect love drives out fear."** There is a mini vision that

I had a few years ago that comes to mind. A vision is a picture that the Lord wants us to see for a specific purpose. In this vision I was on an airport's automatic walkway. I had to go in the opposite direction other than which it was moving. So, in order to get where I was going, I had to dig in some effort to move forward. Occasionally I would stop walking only to have the walkway begin to take me back in the rear direction. I sensed then the Lord saying to me "to keep stopping along faith's journey is equivalent to sliding backward or backsliding". It is not that we need to do a sinful thing that makes us back-slide, just stop moving forward and we will end up there. Our walk of faith is just that a walk not a sprint. When we stop, we just do not stay status quo we actually move slowly backwards.

When I was a young Christian woman I did not understand how much I was loved by God. I have found out that I am smarter than I thought, I am greater than I thought, and I am more resilient than I ever knew. Lean in and listen to this, so are you! I know that nothing can hold me back but me. Just as nothing can hold you back but you. Later in life I was introduced to my favorite poem outside of the Word. I learned it because it was George Washing Carter's favorite poem too;

Equipment
Figure it out for yourself, my lad,
You've all that the greatest of
men have had,
Two arms, two hands, two
legs, two eyes
And a brain to use if you
would be wise.
With this equipment they
all began,
So start for the top and say, "I can."

Look them over, the
wise and great
They take their food from a
common plate,
And similar knives and
forks they use,
With similar laces they tie
their shoes.
The world considers them brave
and smart,
But you've all they had when they
made their start.

You can triumph and come to skill,
You can be great if you only will.
You're well equipped for what fight
you choose,

You have legs and arms and a
brain to use,
And the man who has risen great
deeds to do
Began his life with no
more than you.

You are the handicap you
must face,
You are the one who must choose
your place,
You must say where you
want to go,
How much you will study the
truth to know.
God has equipped you for
life, but He

Lets you decide what you
want to be.

Courage must come from the
soul within,
The man must furnish the
will to win.
So figure it out for yourself, my lad.
You were born with all that the
great have had,
With your equipment they
all began,
Get hold of yourself and
say: "I can."

--Edgar A. Guest

Nothing can hold you back but you. Not the devil, not your sex, not the color of your skin. When you truly receive the love of God, you will say to yourself "I can!" "I am who the Word of God says that I am; I can do what the Word of God says I can do!" That huge fact will keep many people from settling for less just to be accepted. Performance is trying to be what we think someone wants us to be to stay in their good graces. "*The fear of man brings a snare.*" *Proverbs 29:25.*

No longer be bound of what people think of you, no longer allow yourself to be held back by the nay-sayers, the agents of the Hater.

Know that the Lord God loves you. Know that He always finishes what he starts. It is He that is the author and finisher of our faith. The Apostle Paul said this **"Being confident of this very thing, that He which hath begun a good work in you will perform it until the day of Jesus Christ." Phil.1:6** Take hope in the fact that God's Word does not return to Him void. The perfect non-destructible seed of the Word always produces. So, when you feel that you are not enough, keep feeding yourself the

Word of God. That living seed on the inside of you makes you more than enough. The Word of God never comes to the harvest table empty handed. There will always be a bountiful crop if you believe and receive it. (side note- Never compare your crop to another, just rejoice in the bounty that you have received.)

If you grew up as I did and watched the movie "The 10 Commandments" and going to church, you learned the "Thou Shall Not's". So, if you are anything like me, who worked at be pleasing to God you were almost afraid to sin. Believe me, I still did sin and sinned often. It is not that I didn't fail many times but I found that his love is continually constant and never changing towards us. I now know that there is not a thing that I can do to make him stop loving me. When I finally realized how much God loved me, I didn't want to sin nor disappoint the lover of my soul. Our late Pastor George E. Hilton used to say it this way. "I drink all the liquor I want to. I sleep with all the beautiful women that I want to. I smoke all the weed that I want to. Because of my personal love walk with the Father is so great", he would say " I don't want to!" My desire to please Him increases when I think of who He is and how he very much loves me. I love him because he loved me first.

I have often heard people who say that they are believers say things like, "I know that I participate in this or that sin all the time, but God knows my heart." I must agree, God does know our hearts, but he also sees our works. I am not saying that any of us are perfect. However, if we really love God and realized how much we are loved by God, we will walk to please Him in every avenue, even if we should sin. Truly repent and get back up, determined by His power to change. God has supernaturally graced us to live for him. We were saved by grace, but we are empowered by another grace which is God's divine ability to do what he has called us to do. We are graced to be who he called us to be. We have a grace to live in every arena of our life. I can't walk in your grace that it takes for you to successfully live your life just as you cannot walk in mine.

To sin means to miss the bulls-eye on the target. We have all missed the mark, but after a certain span of time with Him and reading His word we ought to be hitting the mark more than missing the mark. We can all use an accountability believer friend. A believing friend is someone you can go to and share your earnest heart and missteps, who will pray for and with you. A true believing friend is someone you know you can trust; you will not hear what you have told them from someone else later. Also, you know that they are not judging you or using what you shared against you at another time. You also need a friend who is not afraid to rebuke you and call you into judgment of yourself. I have a Debbie

Butler for that. We tell each other crazy thoughts and things but we always direct each other back to the Word of God. We listen without judging then pray for one another. Remember love tells the truth.

In the book of Jeremiah God said when we become his, that he will now write his law on our hearts not on a tablet of stone. There was a time that I did not understand that when Jesus came and died in my stead and He paid the way. He fulfilled all of the "Thou shall and shall not's" and that I can enter into his new commandment. Love. *John 13:34 "A new commandment*

I give to you. That you love one another as I have loved you, that ye also love one another." Love is the Ten Commandments in a concise package. If we walked in love, we would not sleep with our neighbor's wife, we would honor our father and mother and we would not take the name of the Lord God in vain, nor murder, nor steal etc. Love is the fulfillment of the law. *Romans 13:10 "...love is the fulfilling of the law."* Jesus is the fulfillment of the Ten Commandments. *Vs.35* goes on to say, by this shall all men know that you belong to me. Our true Love fulfilled the law as an example to follow in Loves footsteps. *I Peter 4:8 "Love covers a multitude of sins.* When we do miss it because none of us are perfect, repent and it is gone. Let the love inside of you be your new sheriff. Fall in love with Love and you will not have a "want to" to sin in you!

Although Christ fulfilled the law there is more in the Old Testament than just the law of Moses. So, we should not throw out the remaining thirty-five books of the Old Testament. There is so much more to be learned from it. Teachings on the heart of the Lord, His likes and dislikes, and how we are to conduct ourselves as believers in this world. The book of Proverbs is for practical wisdom that you could not learn any other place.

When you received what Jesus did for you, know that He also did some things in you. When you accept the love of God and receive Jesus, your once dead spirit is alive and perfect. Our spirit is where our immediate and total salvation has taken place. He has made the real us (our born-again spirit) per-fect. It is our mind that is not per-fected and our bodies that are not perfected. ***Philippians 2:12...work*** *out your own salvation with fear and trembling*. So, from the inside (who you really are your spirit man) to the outside (your body), work it out. We should know that our spirit is where God moved into, but our soul and your body still needs to be redeemed. But know that He will instruct you what to do and what not to do from your inside. Yield to his teaching.

Love is a teacher. Let the Teacher to teach. *Psalm 32:8 "I will instruct thee and teach thee in the way which thou shalt go: I will guide thee with mine eye."* He teaches this is the way, walk ye in it.

Please allow me to translate this verse in my language.

I John 2:27 - the smearing of Love now lives inside of you ... you don't need anyone telling you "thou shall, or thou shall not." Let the Teacher teach! Allow the teacher that now lives inside of you teach you right from wrong. The Holy Spirit of God the 3rd person of the Trinity is called the teacher. Of course, He will always agree with the written Word of God. So, until you learn to discern the teachers leading, be taught by pastors, and teachers who know the Word to help you make wise decisions based on the Bible.

You delve into the Bible and pray and ask God to help you learn and grow up. Pray and find a church where you feel loved and accepted.

I have always loved the color red. When I was a teenager, I always wore red nail polish. So, when I was newly saved and joined a holiness church, my pastor at that time asked me to come into his office one day. He was a strict but old school loving pastor. He said to me, "Please do not let me tell you about wearing that nail polish again." He then pulled out nail polish remover and had me remove it. Gasp! I heard that. You said, "Oh, no he didn't." Now, I laugh hysterically at it. So, I thought to myself, *Okay, if I must be plain old Jane for Jesus, I will.* I stopped wearing makeup and earrings and the rest. Later, when I grew up in the Lord, I learned that the tradition of men making the Word of God has no effect; just a side funny. When our son was a little boy, he came into our bedroom one morning and said, "Who put the wall of mirrors up in the dining room downstairs?" I wondered why he asked, but I answered, "My brother Louis did. Why?" He said, "You should go look in it now to see how atrocious you look in the morning." LOL! I realized makeup and the rest had no bearing on my salvation. I learned that "a little makeup could keep me out of the world book of uglies," as Pastor George once said, but a little makeup won't keep me out of Heaven. LOL! I learned that I have a teacher who lives in me who says yes or no. It is He, that when I would put on something inappropriate, would make the call on the inside. I cannot say I have always listened, but I would be lying if I said I didn't hear. Down on the inside where the Teacher teaches, I hear.

One of my best friends in life is Rhonda. Rhonda and I can tell each other the truth. Whenever we would see someone crazily dressed in wild outfits and such, we would say, "Bless her heart, she ain't got no friends." One time I came to church in a dress that once fit me very nicely, but I had gained weight. Rhonda sent me a text across the church that read, "Girl, you got a friend." LOL! Let the Holy Spirit in you be your teacher and friend. He makes perfect calls.

CHAPTER 6

NO LONGER THE ONLY BEGOTTEN

For Love so loved the world that he gave **His only begotten Son...**" (John 3:16)

God loved us so much that He sacrificed His only at that time, His Son Jesus, to gain us, His many sons and daughters—amazing to even fathom. I as a parent cannot wrap my human mind around such sacrificial love. Imagine along with me. You have one son, only son and you know that the only way to save the world would be to give the life of that only son. Now that son is going to give his life. Yes, give because Jesus said no man takes my life, I lay it down. So, you as a father had to know that some would not honor or respect or reverence your only son nor the awesome sacrifice. To know that his only son was offered up to save humanity, fully knowing that he would be spit on, scorn, hated, and rejected. Jesus was beaten to an unrecognizable pulp for us. Isaiah 52 say that he was beaten till his visage was marred more than any man. In that beating he carried the sin, mental anguish, and sickness for the entire world, then he was ultimately killed. God knew that there was no other way for a sin-sick, seemingly unappreciative world to have a chance at redemption. Knowing fully that some would never except the gift, but rather reject it and spit it back in his face. Love still freely gave Him.

I had to stop writing at this point to sob in the depths of my heart for the wonderful sacrifice and the precious love that God has for me (us). Thank you, Father God.

Would or could you offer your son for such harsh treatment? I honestly could not. I do not even like people not to like my children let alone reject or torture them.

I also could not keep from looking back to Abraham in the Old Testament. Abraham was old and he waited many years to have his promised son born to him and his wife Sarah. Yet, the Lord told him to sacrifice that son in obedience. Abraham, full of faith headed up to the mountain of sacrifice with all the intentions of obeying God. When suddenly the voice of the Lord spoke to him and told him to do his son no harm. Abraham looked up and saw a lamb caught in the thicket. God offered the sacrifice. A shadow of what was to come. The spotless Lamb of God Jesus Christ. God offered the sacrifice in the Old Testament then God offered the sacrifice in the New Testament. That offering will never need to be made ever again. The Word said that Jesus once and for all was slain.

I hate to think it, but I may have had excuses why not to offer my son. "I must have heard wrong." "I need to fast certain days to know for sure." on and on and on.

Jesus was born to die. Jesus, the spotless Lamb of God, was prepared and slain from the foundation of the world. God was fulfilling His plan for us through him. Now, Jesus died and rose again, and we too are raised with Him. We are raised from our spiritually dead state with Jesus. Whether we know it, we were all dead in our trespasses and sins until Jesus. We are now sons and daughter in a huge family if we have accepted the love freely given.

When we accepted what Jesus did for us and we asked him to live in us and come into our heart, we were adopted. We were adopted into the royal family. I thought about adoption, how you cannot *un-adopt* someone after the adoption process is complete. As baby Christians, we get adopted before we are adapted to the ways of God. But know that your adoption is complete, and the documents have all been signed in the court of heaven. Our names have been written down in the book of life. The Word of God says that we are sealed with the Holy Spirit of promise. We are forever in God's heart. You cannot lose your salvation, but you can reject it if you want.

I then thought about the royal family. When Princess Diana and Prince Charles were divorced, she lost her official title of Her Royal Highness (HRH) and many other things. From reading, I understand that that alone caused her so much pain. She went from Her Royal Highness to Diana the Princess of Wales. Her son Prince William vowed that he would restore her title when he became king. After the divorce, she was then required to bow to other royals. How humiliating that had to be. Sadly, we know of her tragic end.

I thought about Meghan Markle, who became Her Royal Highness too. When she and Harry stepped down from their positions, she took on the title of the Duchess of Sussex and no longer HRH.

Then I thought about our position in Christ and through his precious blood, how we have been adopted into the royal family, not married in. We are His Royal Highness's children. We are permanent members if we choose to stay.

We are His and He is ours, forever. Never again do you need to fear being left or rejected or abandoned.

> For he hath said, I will never leave thee nor forsake thee. So that we may boldly say, The Lord is my helper, and I will not fear what man shall do unto me. (Hebrews 13:5)

Say it with me: "LOVE loves me!" Now boldly say, "The Lord is my helper." There is a difference between saying and boldly saying. Boldly means with confidence, knowing to whom you belong. You know that you are a King's kid and have no problem coming to the throne to approach your Daddy. The blood of Jesus gives us boldness. We cannot overload our heavenly Father, who loves us and always has time for us. He always has an ear open to us.

Take confidence in that "He said SO THAT WE CAN BOLDLY SAY!" Faith says something. Your faith in God and His Word should have the last word.

I strongly believe in daily confessions and affirmations. From the moment that I open my eyes in the morning, I speak. You win victory over a thought with your words. I say what I believe based on the Word of God, morning till night. I know that it has been said that we are the "blab it and grab it" group. If you are wise, you are not just blabbing and grabbing. But you should be boldly saying because He said something first. I have made it my habit to blab and grab all that He said I can have. I blab and grab who He says that I am. I blab and grab what I believe for my health, wealth, and soundness and always according to what Love has already said.

CHAPTER 7

WHO'S A WHOSOEVER?

For God so loved the world that he gave his only begotten son, that whoso-ever *believes in him...*

You are a whosoever if you choose to be one. I have people who say to me I don't believe in God;

I often answer, God believes in you though. Regardless of whether you choose to receive it, Love will keep on loving you. My prayer is that you have seized the gift.

It is at the cross of Jesus where there is no longer a distinction between man or woman, child or adult, black or white, Jew or gentile. The work of the cross is for whosoever will receive it. No one can make that decision for you to believe but you. Your parents nor grandparent's relationship with the Lord cannot speak for you. I have heard it said that God does not have grandchildren. You must come to him as your personal Father on your very own. One day when we all stand before Him (and we all will), there will be no excuses of parents.

> For there is no differ-
> ence between Jew and
> Greek: for the same
> Lord unto all is rich unto
> all that call upon him.
> (Romans 10:12)

> There is neither Jew nor
> Greek there is neither
> bond nor free there is
> neither male nor female

for you are all one in Christ. (Galatians 3:28)

We are all equal at the cross of Calvary. I have met other ministers who think that their title puts them up above others in the body of Christ. I have met professionals who think that they are what they do in this life. We shall all stand before the judgment seat of Christ to give an account of our lives before Him. The only thing that would make a difference will be whether you believed the gift that was freely given to all, Jesus.

"At the cross where I first saw the light and the burdens of my heart rolled away, it was there by faith I received my sight and now I am happy all the day."-(Lyrics ~ Isaac Watts, 1674-1748)

For God so loved the world that he gave his only begotten son that **whosoever** *believes* in *him should not perish.*

Believes. Believes what? That God is the Most High. Believe that

Jesus is his son, who came to die in our stead. Believe that God raised him from the dead. Believe that we are now justified because of his bloodshed for us. Believe that we have been raised with him. Believe that Love loves you.

I remember some years back that I was the speaker at a weekend retreat. I spoke on Friday night, then three times on Saturday, and then again on Sunday morning before we all departed for home. I had preached, prophesied, taught, sang, and prayed for everyone there. The Lord, as he always does, met us in a glorious way. When we were leaving, I was exhausted. I felt like I needed a retreat to recoup from the retreat.

So my thought was on the hour-and-a-half ride home I will just sleep. As I settled into sleep, I heard THE VOICE say, "Call Norma. Tell her there is a difference between believing and receiving." Well, Norma is a good friend of mine and was in one of the other cars making their way back home from the retreat too. So I made myself wake up to obey THE VOICE.

I got out my cell phone and called Norma. I told her what the Lord said to me. We both knew it was about a house that she was believing for. When I gave her the word, she received it and said, "Father, I receive it in Jesus's name." By the time we returned home, the house was hers! Glory to God! Remember, faith says something, faith has a voice.

There are many who believe that there is a higher power, they believe that God is real, they believe there is a heaven and hell. But your believing is powerless until you utilize your will and receive what you believe. That is the thing that we need to understand. Our will after this life does not hold the same power or authority that it does right now on earth. When you step out of this life and you haven't chosen Jesus, you face hell and then you want to decide that you have changed your mind and now want to make a choice for Jesus, but it will be too late. Your human will has the power of choice while in your body here on earth. When you step over into the other side, you have already sealed your eternity. Receiving by faith is done with your words. Practice saying, "I believe that, and I receive that in Jesus's name." When you hear the evil report, start saying, I don't believe that, and I don't receive that, I refuse it in Jesus's name. I believe and agree with what the Word of God has already said.

> That if thou shalt confess with thy mouth the Lord Jesus and believe in thine heart that God has raised him from the dead thou shalt be saved. (Romans 10:9)

Believe and receive

> For with the heart man believes and with the

mouth is made con-
fession unto salvation.
(Romans 10:10)

If you believe, use your mouth to
receive for anything and everything
that you are trusting God for.

There is no reason to ever wait
to pray to the Father God. He is
as close as your breath. Remember,
faith is now. We never have to go to
a man, nor wait until Sunday to get
to a certain building to pray. Why?
Because God lives inside of us and is
omnipresent. Omnipresent means
He is everywhere, always. What
an amazing God. If now is when

you believe, now is a great time to receive any and everything that you need from the Lord. If healing is what you need, ask in faith now; if peace is what you need, ask Him now. Whatever you may have need of, know that nothing is too big for Him to handle or too hard for Him to do. Believe and receive. You might say I want to believe, but how do I believe? Faith is just that, faith. Faith is trusting that if God said it in his Word, it is true. Faith comes by hearing the Word of God. Then it is a choice to agree with God. God is a gentleman and can totally be trusted, his Word is good. Begin to speak what you believe based on the Bible. God backs his Word—it never comes back void.

CHAPTER 8

A DEBT OF LOVE

Love's fruit will manifest in countless ways, giving, forgiving, feeding, clothing, being compassionate, and on and on.

The love of God is shed abroad in our hearts by the Holy Ghost. (Romans 5:5)

We are slathered inside with Love.

We owe what we have been saturated in, but we must release it. The Bible says:

> To whom much is given much is required. (Luke 12:48)

We are commanded to love others. We owe love because our Great God has been so very gracious to us to give us an unlimited supply to share.

Uh, Oh. I feel another song coming on. "I owe, I owe, a debt of love to sow."

The Word of God says:

Owe nothing to anyone except to love and seek the best for one another; for he who [unselfishly] loves his neighbor has fulfilled the [essence of the] law [relating to one's fellowman]. (Romans 13:8)

Thou shalt love the Lord thy God with all thy heart, and with all thy soul, and with all thy mind.

This is the first and great commandment.

And the second [is] like unto it, Thou shalt love thy neighbour as thyself. (Matthew 22:37–40)

There have been times when we will not necessarily like someone; however, we are instructed to walk in God's love with them. I like most people, but I must admit there are those who right down irk me. That is where we have to strive to be like Him. I did not say it is always easy, I am just saying that it is doable. I am a person too. At times I gotta reach down inside of me past the me to the overflowing reserve that has been extended to me and pull love up and pay it forward. Love is a command.

I have a girlfriend named Jinx (aka Prophetess Regina Astheimer), who is so full of the love of God. She will put someone in their place and then turn around and feed their entire family. She does not tolerate foolishness for a moment, she will rebuke whoever needs it sharply and then will give to them over and above just to bless them and meet their needs. During her own challenging times she has gone out of her way to clothe, feed, nurture, counsel countless people. I cannot remember a time after speaking to her that she hangs up without saying, "Do you all need anything?" The counsel that she offers is always consistent with the Word. Some of the people that she gives to don't even know what her name is; when they see her coming into their neighborhood they say, "That church lady is here" as she comes to feed their families. One time I went to a hairdressers 40 miles from where she lives. I met a woman who was telling me that she was moving into Jinx's area, so I told her I have a friend that will help get her on her feet and acclimated to the community. I laughed when she responded that she had recently met her and had married into her family. She affirmed that, yes, Jinx is just who I had said she was. What an awesome testimony of the love of God.

Beloved, if God so loved
us, we ought also to love
one another. (I John 4:11)

I thought about a good friend of mine who is kind of to herself and quiet. She told me how there were those who right down ignored her until they found that she was a good friend of mine. Suddenly, some who she tried to speak to many times went out of their way to be noticed by her. I had to share with her not to feel bad. I have had a certain neighbor many years ago who daily turned up her nose and would not speak to me. One day she heard me speak and then realized who I was. Then she came to one of my conferences, and everything changed. Oh, the phoniness, yuck! The book of Jude speaks of being in admiration of men's persons. We are not to love people based on what they have or who we think they are or can do for us. That is not love. Love is loving those who are not lovely too.

Let love be without dis-simulation. (Romans 12:9

Don't ever let your love be insincere or phony. Love because God is real, and God is love. Love as though you are entertaining one of God's angels, because you never know when you really might be doing so.

Love without partiality, love without hypocrisy, love others in return for the fact that you are loved.

CHAPTER 9

NEVER ALONE AGAIN

For God so loved the world that he gave his only begotten Son, that whosoever believes in him should not perish but have *everlasting life.* (John 3:16)

What do the phrases ever-lasting or eternal life mean? Does it mean that I will I walk around this earth when I am 853 years old? What is this eternal life about? To have everlasting life means that here into eternity, you will live with God. Everlasting life started the moment that you prayed the prayer to receive Jesus. God lives inside of your heart forever. "Everlasting" and "eternal" is the Greek word aionios it means past and future, without beginning or end, always will be and never ceasing. You now have a brand-new life with Him. It speaks of a brand-new relationship with God himself. You do not cease to exist when you close your eyes in earthly death. Your relationship with God never will end, here or in heaven itself. The Bible refers to hell as the second death. Hell is eternal separation from Love. Some say that we are living in hell. No matter how bad you may have had it in this life, you have no idea how good you have had it in comparison to an eternal hell. The Word of God says in Hebrews 9:27, "...it is appointed unto men once to die, but after this the judgment." If you receive Love, you will never experience what the

Bible refers to as the second death in the judgment.

> Then the LORD God took the man and put him in the garden of Eden to tend and keep it. And the LORD God commanded the man, saying, "Of every tree of the garden you may freely eat; but of the tree of the knowledge of good and evil you shall not eat, for in the day that you eat of it you shall surely die." (Genesis 2:15–17)

In the original Hebrew it is written, "And in dying you shall die." Die and then die.

God clearly stated: "*For in the day*" of disobedience to My instruction, the death process will begin. And it did! Adam did not fall over that day and stopped breathing, but death of his spirit happened, and then his human shell eventually caught up. So Adam died and then died. With that, Adam entered into a covenant with Satan and basically signed over dominion of the earth to him. With that, he gave him the legal deed with the rights to rule. From then, the curse began, things died, sickness came, fires, horrible storms and every and any other evil thing you can imagine. These are the things that many times get attributed to God. Even insurance policies say things like an "act of God." Part of being a born-again child of God is taking back the dominion that was once lost. By reigning as God's kids on this earth, we take back what the enemy of our souls took through Adam.

The absolute best way for me to describe eternal life is starting from the very moment that one accepts the love of the Lord: we will never again be separated from LOVE.

For God so personally and passionately loves you that He offered the life of His only Son Jesus on the torturous cross of Calvary: that if you would only believe that he did it just for you, you will never die but have a full, wonderful life of love, relationship with fellowship with Him forever, here on earth and forevermore in heaven.

> God did not send Jesus in the world to convict, condemn nor criticize it but that the world through him might be saved. (John 3:17)

God sometimes gets a bad rap throughout the world. He gets blamed for the work of the Hater. People tell lies on God of how he destroyed their life to help keep them humble or things like God gets glory when out of sickness. If that is true, why would we go against God's glory and take medicines or go to a doctor? Here is one that I have heard at funerals. God needed another angel in heaven. God did not pen the movie The Body Snatchers to get more angels on his staff. Plus, people do not become angels. According to Genesis 1:26 we are made in the

likeness and class of God. Angels
are a lower class than we are, and we
will never be moved down to angel
class. No matter how it looks in one
of my favorite Christmas movies,
(Frank Capra's) It's a Wonderful
Life. Remember Love loves you;
the Hater hates you.

The best way to get to know
about the love of God toward you
is to read what His Word, the Bible,
has to say to you. Read your Bible,
and see how time after time, God
bought nothing but victory for his
obedient children. Not one battle
lost, not one turned away empty,
not one of his kids begging bread,

never, never, never. Wow, what a record! I choose to trust and believe.

The apostle Paul said this is the reason that he bowed his knee to God his Father.

Only Jesus has the power to save! His name is the only one in all the world that can save anyone. Acts 4:12 CEV If you are in the family, we all came in through the same door, faith in Him. Jesus is the door. The Bible says that there is no other door to the Father but through the Son Jesus. A person cannot follow what they want to be true and add this belief to the Word of God. Syncretism is attempting to mix and match religious beliefs and attributing them to the true God. We also do not get to cherry-pick which parts we like in the Bible and then ignore the parts that we don't. We have been bought with the precious blood of Jesus. We need to know that we now belong to Him. I know many try to say that there are many paths to God. Lie told! The Bible goes onto say in John 10:1 that if any tries to come in another way, that that man is a thief and a liar.

That he would grant you, according to the riches of

**his glory, to be strength-
ened with might by his
Spirit in the inner man.
That Christ may dwell
in your heart by faith;
that ye, being rooted
and grounded in love.
(Ephesians 3:16–17)**

The root base and the soil that
we are planted into is Love himself. We need to come to know how
wide, long, deep, and high the love
of God extends for and to us.

**May be able to compre-
hend with all the saints**

what is the breadth, and the length, and depth and height; And to know (become intimately acquainted with Love) the love of Christ which passes (head) knowledge, that ye might be filled with all the fulness of God. (Ephesians 3:18–19)

I especially like the phrase in Paul's prayer above for the church, "To know the love of Christ." It is the Greek word **ginosko**, which means to absolutely know. Know the Anointed One and his anointing that lives in us. Just think the God of the universe wants us to be so entangled with Him intimately that children are bought forth. Our love story with the Lord ought to produce life, for him, for us, and for others.

When we receive Him, He is always present with us. Never a moment of the day goes by that you need to be absent of his love and presence.

When I think on all the great things that he has done, I cannot help but to want to praise and thank Him. Worship must be from your heart. As you grow in fellowship, it is only natural to want to praise him. Just start out by thanking him, thank him for everything that you can think of that is good in your life. Write a list, I bet you will run out of paper before you run out of praises. Get a gratitude journal and daily jot down a few things that you appreciate. Complain less, praise more.

Be thankful unto Him and bless His name for the Lord is good. (Psalm 100:4–5)

Be thankful for your family, your spouse, your sight, and hearing, a sunny day. Praise him often, it does not have to be at prayer time, but anytime. The Bible said that as you praise, you stop the devil's activity in your life. Praise paralyzes the Hater. Thank God for everything that you have, your home, family, car, your job. I forget where I heard this recently, but it was said, "Praise is a magnet for miracles." There was a song out when I was younger that said, "Don't wait until the battle is over, shout now." Praise in advance of what you are believing God to do in your future. Go ahead, give a shout of praise. Hallelujah, thank you, Jesus!

Do you remember when you were a child and you would pick a daisy or some sort of flower and play this game, "He loves me, he loves me not, he loves me, he loves me not"? We would play that game always wishing to end on "He loves me." With God you will never ever have a need to play that game again. Regardless of whether a man, a woman, a person loves you or not, you are and always will be loved. Always remember that Love will always love you. So this is how I play this game now. He loves me, he loves me, he loves me, he loves me. LOVE loves me! Love always wins. There is no failure in His love, for Love never fails.

I could write volumes of how God loves us, but I cannot end without adding these last two passages of scripture. Please take your time with each, read them slowly and aloud. Soak in them and let them sink into your heart and mind.

Who shall separate us from the love of Christ?
Shall tribulation?
Distress?
Persecution?

Famine?
Nakedness?
Peril?
Sword?
As it is written
For thy sake we are killed
all day long;
We are accounted as sheep for
the slaughter
Nay, in all these things we are
more than conquerors
Through him that loved us
For I am persuaded that neither
Death
Life
Angels
Principalities

Nor powers
Nor things present
Nor things to come
No height
Nor depth
Nor any other creature
shall be able to separate us from
the love of God,
which is in Christ Jesus our Lord.
(Romans 8:35)

Love is patient. Love is kind.
Love isn't jealous. It doesn't sing
its own praises. It isn't arrogant.
It isn't rude. It doesn't think
about itself. It isn't irritable. It
doesn't keep track of wrongs.

It isn't happy when injustice is done, but it is happy with the truth. Love never stops being patient, never stops believing, never stops hoping, never gives up. Love never comes to an end. (I Corinthians 13:4–8 GW)

Now re-read that 1rst Corinthians 13 again. Exchange the word love and the word it with your personal name. Strive to conduct yourself in that same way daily. When you have missed the mark, confess it and by God's ability in you, just do better the next time.

I love you and thank you for going on this journey of Love with me.

Know this, that no matter where you go in this life, LOVE is with you. Also know that no matter what you face, LOVE is pulling for you. So, live your life as though LOVE himself is watching over you because He is.

One last thing...

I would like to invite you to join with me daily in part of my confession of faith:

LOVE loves me
LOVE loves people
I love LOVE

LOVE loves through me
LOVE abounds in me richly
I am LOVE'S vessel
I walk in LOVE
I talk in LOVE
I live LOVE

For thine O Lord is the greatness
And the power and the glory and
the victory and the majesty.
For all that is in heaven and
earth is thine.

This is the day of the glory of God,
And I believe to see the miracu-
lous power of God manifested in
my life, today and every day!

So, I ask you again.
What's love got to do with it?
EVERYTHING!

ABOUT THE AUTHOR

Dee Williams perceived her call to the ministry around the early age of 12. After publicly acknowledging her salvation many years later she began to do whatever her hands could find to do for the Lord. She was later ordained to ministry. Realizing that knowledge puffs up, but love builds up she always honors the privilege of being allowed of the Lord to speak at various churches, conferences, and retreats. She has also copy-written over 79 worship songs to the Lord. Alongside of her husband of 35 years, she has co-founded The House of the Restored Church in conjunction with Saturday Night Thrive and Iron 2 Iron Ministry

Dee can be reached for speaking engagements on her Facebook page Saturday Night Thrive Email at
Lovelovesme.1@gmail.com
&
Preachdee@gmail.com